SELF

SELF

*A Reflective Collection of
Poems for Self-Betterment*

MICHAEL VJ CONNELLY

First edition

ISBN: 979-8-9940109-1-4 (paperback)
ISBN: 979-8-9940109-0-7 (e-book)

CONTENTS

DEDICATION

For my mother, Silvana Ludovici. She came from Nettuno, just outside of Rome, carrying with her the endurance and quiet pride of our Roman heritage.

Silvana Ludovici, 1959

INTRODUCTION

I am not an expert in self-improvement or wellness. I am a human pilot, navigating a lifelong journey toward self-betterment. For years, I was caught in turbulence — a twenty-year, unhappy marriage with my ex-wife, and a career that left me consumed by tunnel vision. The emotions of past experiences controlled me; each memory carried pain, mistrust, or unhappiness. I brought that turbulence home, and it weighed on my ability to give focus, time, and attention to my current wife and the people who mattered most. Over time, I began to contemplate the way prior experiences trigger emotions — and the possibility of separating the two. I learned, slowly, how to pause, breathe, and think. How to dissociate a feeling from the event that caused it. An event, after all, can simply remain in the past — unless we allow it to keep wounding us in the present. In this practice, I discovered the beginnings of peace, gratitude, and self-reflection. Poetry came to me almost unexpectedly. Each day, I drove an hour and a half to and from work, time I once considered wasted. But in that space, I found room to think. One morning, as I reflected on how grateful I was to have my wife beside me — to share successes, challenges, and the simple act of working through life together — I realized what a gift this is, to humanity. From that thought, my first poem, A Brilliant Light in Humanity, was born. That was the moment I discovered a creative side I never knew existed. I came to understand that progress is rarely linear — it moves like the ocean, receding and flowing with time. In that rhythm, my poems became anchors: reflections I could return to, guiding me back on course and reminding me, as a human pilot, to stay steady on the lifelong journey of self-betterment.

This book is dedicated to my mother, Silvana Ludovici. She came from Nettuno, just outside of Rome — carrying with her the strength, endurance, and quiet pride of her Roman heritage. That strength was her gift to me. My mother worked two jobs, carrying exhaustion on her shoulders, yet still managed to give in ways that reflected pure love. I remember Christmas especially. After long hours at work, she would fill our home with the aroma of food — not just for her children, but for the neighbors as well. The table overflowed with a delicious variety of dishes she had made, each one prepared with care, as though love itself were one of the ingredients. Though she had little, she gave much. Though time was scarce, she created moments of abundance. In her, I witnessed resilience, sacrifice, and generosity. She endured hardship with quiet strength but never allowed the weight of life to rob her of the ability to give joy. Her example taught me that love is not diminished by struggle; in fact, it often grows deeper through it. My mother never had the opportunity to focus on her own self-betterment — she was too busy surviving, providing, and nurturing. And yet, she embodied its essence daily: through her commitment, her compassion, and her ability to make others feel valued and cared for. This book, in many ways, is a reflection of what she modeled for me. It is also a tribute to the Roman pillar that is part of my heritage — a reminder that strength and resilience are not only personal traits, but part of the legacy we carry forward. The poems, reflections, and exercises you will find here are not only for me, but for her and for anyone who has ever carried unspoken battles while still choosing to love.

1

GRATITUDE AND PURPOSE

This collection of poems explores the transformative power of gratitude, purpose, and connection. The poems and reflections invite you to consider how recognizing the light in ourselves and others can deepen our sense of meaning and belonging. Through celebrating shared journeys, acts of selflessness, and the importance of loving relationships, we are reminded that life's greatest gifts often lie in our connections with one another. Let these words guide you to notice the brilliance in humanity — both in your own heart and in the bonds you create.

A BRILLIANT LIGHT IN HUMANITY

"Love does not consist in gazing at each other, but in looking outward together in the same direction."

— Antoine de Saint-Exupéry

Each individual follows a journey toward purpose, passion, and happiness.

Another who strives for the same, creating two unique worlds independently.

But oh, what a gift — a brilliant light in humanity — when the two join, creating one love, one love shared, fluently, expressing to each other their life missions that make them the best version of themselves.

Sharing their success, happiness, and challenges along their journey.

But what a gift, brilliant light in humanity, a unity that supports, loves, encourages, and helps pave a path to one's life goals, dreams, and happiness.

A priceless part of life — joining and creating a lifetime of cyclical connection from two to one.

Oh, what a brilliant light in humanity.

REFLECTION

The poem "A Brilliant Light in Humanity" captures what I feel is the essence of human connection and the profound impact it has on our lives. It begins by acknowledging the individuality of each person's journey toward their own purpose, passion, and happiness. This recognition of personal growth and self-discovery sets the stage for the poem's central theme: the transformative power of unity. When two individuals, each on their own unique path, come together, they create something extraordinary. The poem describes this union as a "brilliant light in humanity," highlighting the beauty and significance of shared love and mutual support. This connection allows them to express their life missions fluently, helping each other become the best versions of themselves. The poem emphasizes that this shared journey is not just about the good times but also about supporting each other through challenges, thus creating a bond that is both deep and resilient. I repeat the phrase "brilliant light in humanity" to reinforce the idea that such connections are rare and precious. The poem suggests that this unity is a priceless part of life, one that brings immense joy and fulfillment. It speaks to the cyclical nature of this connection, where two individuals continuously support and uplift each other, creating a lifetime of shared experiences and growth. In essence, the poem is a celebration of the power of love and unity. It reminds us that while our individual journeys are important, the connections we make with others can bring an unparalleled brilliance to our lives. The poem underscores the importance of cherishing and nurturing the relationships that bring light and meaning to our existence.

PRACTICAL EXERCISES

Gratitude and Purpose

JOURNALING PROMPT

Reflect on a relationship in your life that brings light and meaning. Write about how this connection has supported your growth and what you value most about it.

GRATITUDE PRACTICE

Each morning for a week, list three things or people you are grateful for and explain why. Notice how this shifts your outlook during the day.

REFLECTION QUESTION

How can you be a "brilliant light" for someone else? What small acts of support or encouragement could you offer today?

THE DAY THAT THE WORLD STOOD STILL

"The most precious gift we can offer anyone is our attention."

— Thich Nhat Hanh

The noise of the world distracts the heart and mind — unmindful of others in this moment in time.

Attention not given — my wife's words unheard — for my focus was within.

Within my own mind — though unintentional — is seemingly unkind.

Suddenly, the noise of the world, its distractions paused, not a planned event, but I understand the cause. Amidst it all, acts of caring and thoughtfulness my wife gives to me, not from her happiness in the moment for this I can see.

It's from the love in her heart that's given to me. Given to me unconditionally.

The acts that made the world stand still make me stop and realize what is important in my life — the one I love, my wife.

Love for all the things, selflessness in her nature, no matter the state of the world or what it brings.

Reflecting on this, I have learned I must give the same to her in return.

So when the noise of the world brings distractions, I will stop the world with my loving, selfless actions.

I will do this by remembering what is important in my life, the one I love, that is my wife.

REFLECTION

I wanted to capture the essence of love, mindfulness, and the importance of appreciating the significant people in our lives. It begins by illustrating the distractions and noise of the world that often divert our attention away from those we care about. I acknowledge that, in moments of self-absorption, I can unintentionally neglect my spouse's words and feelings, which can come across as unkind. However, the turning point in the poem occurs when the distractions of the world suddenly pause. This unplanned moment of clarity allows me to recognize the acts of caring and thoughtfulness that my spouse consistently offers. These acts are not driven by immediate happiness but stem from a deep, unconditional love. This realization makes me stop and reflect on what truly matters in life — the love and selflessness of my spouse. The poem emphasizes the transformative power of love and the importance of reciprocating it. It helps me learn I must give the same selfless love in return, especially when the world's distractions threaten to take over. By committing to stopping the world with loving actions, I vow to prioritize my spouse and remember what is truly important.

In essence, "The Day That the World Stood Still" is a heartfelt reflection on the significance of love and mindfulness in our relationships. It reminds us to cherish and reciprocate the selfless acts of those we love, even amidst the chaos and noise of the world.

This reflection underscores the poem's message that true love is about being present, attentive, and appreciative of the ones.

PRACTICAL EXERCISES

Love and Presence

JOURNALING PROMPT

Recall a recent moment when someone showed you love or patience in a difficult time. How did it feel, and how might you "stop the world" for someone you love?

MINDFUL LISTENING EXERCISE

For your next conversation with someone close, place all distractions aside. Listen with openness and attention, repeating back what you've heard before responding.

REFLECTION QUESTION

What simple act could you offer today to express your appreciation to someone important in your life?

HEARTBEAT OF A UNION

"What you do speaks so loudly that I cannot hear what you say."

— Ralph Waldo Emerson

The practice of patience opens heart and mind to listening without judgment or anger, each will find.

Perspective of the others experiences, feelings, thoughts is gained by seeing through their eyes. Emotional selfishness, each shall refrain.

Gratefulness as a ritual to remember to remind, the goodness in actions of each over time.

Such memories are priceless treasures — the mental gold — for each in the union they now hold.

A learned understanding commitment achieved — to give love in the way it is best received.

Affection is shared through physical touch — hand and face intertwined in a warm embrace.

Forming a bond in silence, nothing heard, creating a union without spoken word.

Each in the union is observant and sees how busy and burdensome life can be.

Excellence and practice both shall be in acts of service in balance, for it is key.

Attentiveness to valued acts — to alleviate, contribute, and support — is sustained. Through the days, weeks, months, and years, commitment to actions shall remain.

Precious is the quality of time — absolute in both heart and mind.

Consistent are the moments meaningful, true, recognized, and valued by each of the two.

Actions continuous, strong, and true, showing unity, selflessness, shall embody the two.

An enduring cycle shall achieve creation of rhythm, a heartbeat of the union each believes.

For the strength of the heartbeat shall define the longevity of union through the test of time.

REFLECTION

"Heartbeat of a Union" is a celebration of the qualities that make a relationship strong and enduring. It reminds me of the importance of patience, understanding, gratefulness, affection, and commitment in creating a lasting bond. The poem aims to capture the essence of a union that is built on mutual respect, support, and love, and highlights the significance of these qualities in sustaining a relationship through the challenges and joys of life.

Relationship Reflection

JOURNALING PROMPT

Describe the qualities you value most in your closest relationship. How do you contribute to the "heartbeat" of this union?

ACTION STEP

Choose one act of service or appreciation to offer your loved one this week. Write about the experience and any changes you notice in your relationship.

REFLECTION QUESTION

In what ways can you practice greater patience and gratitude in your relationships?

2

MINDFULNESS AND PRESENCE

This collection of poems invites you into the world of mindfulness, presence, and selfawareness. The poems explore how pausing, breathing, and paying attention can transform our experience of daily life. They reflect on the power of thoughtful language, the importance of living in the present, and the ongoing process of overcoming self-doubt. Let these words encourage you to observe your thoughts and feelings with compassion, cultivate presence, and discover the strength that comes from accepting yourself fully in each moment.

SHHH...PAUSE...
BREATHE...THINK

Between stimulus and response, there is a space. In that space is our power to choose our response."

— Viktor E. Frankl

Spoken words you cannot retract — stern, reactive, and heavy in their impact.

Impact like rock to water rippling will transcend outward, onward, cannot stop, cannot end.

SSHHH … Pause … Breathe…. Think

A fictional reality through mind's' mistruths created by quick judgement true meaning dilutes.

A piece of the whole judgment is made. True understanding lost, true meaning fades.

SHHH … Pause … Breathe … Think

Pause for perspective for what's at hand, observe not the piece but the whole to truly understand.

To understand a situation, a person, a feeling inside, to remove the mistruths in your mind.

REFLECTION

"SHHH … Pause … Breathe … Think" is a reflection on the importance of mindfulness, empathy, and thoughtful communication. It reminds us to take a moment to pause and consider the impact of our words and actions, striving for true understanding and meaningful connections with others. This reflection underscores the poem's message that by being mindful and intentional in our interactions, we can create a more compassionate and understanding world.

When we pause, even for a breath, we interrupt the automatic reactions that often guide our words. In that small moment of awareness, we create space — space to choose intention over impulse, clarity over confusion, and understanding over assumption. This space becomes a doorway into emotional awareness, offering us the chance to respond with greater patience and humanity.

Mindfulness invites us to recognize that our first interpretation of a situation is not always the full truth. Our minds can distort meaning through past experiences, fear, or misunderstandings. The act of pausing allows us to widen our perspective, to step outside the narrow lens of our immediate emotions and instead view what is happening with a more balanced and compassionate mindset.

When we take time to breathe deeply, we ground ourselves. The breath anchors the present moment and quiets the noise of the world long enough for us to hear what truly matters — the sincerity in someone's voice, the weight behind their words, the intention beneath their expression. In that stillness, we regain the ability to listen, not just with our ears but with understanding.

Thinking — the final step — does not mean overthinking or spiraling into doubt. Instead, it is a mindful evaluation: What is really being said? What am I feeling? What is the most compassionate response I can offer? This conscious reflection strengthens emotional resilience and improves the quality of our relationships.

Practicing this sequence regularly helps us develop a more thoughtful presence in the world. It teaches us to move through conversations with awareness, reducing misunderstandings and encouraging connection. Over time, this practice becomes a quiet discipline — a commitment to showing up with intention rather than reacting from habit.

Ultimately, "SHHH ... Pause ... Breathe ... Think" is an invitation. It asks us to slow down, to observe ourselves honestly, and to cultivate the inner stillness required to communicate with clarity and kindness. It encourages us to navigate life with a gentler spirit, strengthening the bridges we build with others and the compassion we extend to ourselves.

Mindful Communication

JOURNALING PROMPT

Think of a recent conversation where you spoke or reacted impulsively. What might you have said or done differently with a pause?

BREATHING EXERCISE

Before responding in challenging moments, practice the "Shhh... Pause...Breathe...Think" sequence. Notice how it changes your response.

REFLECTION QUESTION

How can you foster greater understanding and empathy in your daily interactions?

MY ENEMY MY SELF

"You have power over your mind — not outside events. Realize this, and you will find strength."

— Marcus Aurelius

Excuse me — do I have your attention? Good.

It's another start to the day: a mental wardrobe, dark or gray.

The morning menu looks the same — indulgence in past tribulations and self-blame, the negative in humanity will complete the meal, even though you know how it makes you feel.

This ritual sets in motion the course of the day. No thought of the present — come what may. Only the past and future in mind's eye guide the day.

Do I still have your attention? I still have much to say, man in the mirror, I know you cannot look away. Tomorrow, tomorrow is a different day.

No, no, no discussion nor debate allow me to further articulate. You will no longer use emotional currency to lease negative thoughts nor prior pain.

Time to change. Time to gain a better version of self through living in the present with a positive mind and negative thoughts shall be left behind.

So tomorrow's mental wardrobe shall be crisp, and bright, as things will be manifested in a positive light.

Morning menu, you shall find healthy for the spirit and the mind. Full of positive thoughts and affirmations.

Living in the present completes the meal, and yes, I do know and look forward to how it will make me feel.

REFLECTION

The poem "My Enemy My Self" delves into the internal struggle many of us face with negative thoughts and self-blame. It begins by emphasizing the repetitive nature of starting each day with a "mental wardrobe" filled with dark or gray thoughts. It describes how indulging in past tribulations and self-blame sets the tone for the day, with the mind fixated on the past and future rather than the present. The turning point in the poem comes when it addresses the "man in the mirror," urging a shift in mindset. It declares that tomorrow will be different, emphasizing the need to stop using "emotional currency" to dwell on negative thoughts and past pain. This powerful metaphor suggests that we have the choice to invest our emotional energy in more positive and constructive ways. The poem then envisions a brighter future, where the "mental wardrobe" is filled with positivity and the "morning menu" is healthy for both the spirit and mind. It highlights the importance of living in the present, filled with positive thoughts and affirmations. This shift in mindset is portrayed as a transformative experience, one that we can look forward to with anticipation. In essence, "MY ENEMY MY SELF" is a reflection on the power of mindset and the importance of living in the present. It encourages us to break free from the cycle of negative thoughts and self-blame, and to embrace a more positive and mindful approach to life.

The poem serves as a reminder that we have the power to change our thoughts. In doing so, we change the course of our day, and ultimately, our lives.

PRACTICAL EXERCISES

Self-awareness and Mindset

JOURNALING PROMPT

What recurring negative thought patterns do you notice in your mornings? Write about how you might shift these habits for a more positive start.

DAILY AFFIRMATION PRACTICE

Each morning, write one positive affirmation to repeat throughout your day.

REFLECTION QUESTION

When you catch yourself dwelling on the past or worrying about the future, what strategies help you return to the present?

I SHALL REMAIN

I can be changed by what happens to me.
But I refuse to be reduced by it."

— Maya Angelou

Life is a cycle that changes and recurs, as with nature, this is true through each transition, I shall remain to see things through.

With loved ones through their cycle of change. Steadfast, to support, be confident, and patient, I shall remain.

My stance is not limited to others — it includes myself. Not to fret in times in life I can contemplate nature and its strife.

As in winter — trees stand stark and bare, through the cold winter wind and frost of air.

Summer's heat turns green to brown, dry and brittle leaves and plants wilt and fall to the ground.

Oh, but do not fret for their roots are steadfast and remain waiting for a time of change.

For in time brings warmth and rain, allowing roots to sustain.

Turning brown to green, the plants grow tall — with vibrant colors again to be seen.

Like the roots, I will be steadfast. I shall remain, for life's cycle will bring things to sustain.

REFLECTION

"I shall Remain" focuses on capturing the essence of resilience and steadfastness in the face of life's cyclical changes. It begins by drawing a parallel between the cycles of nature and the cycles of human life, emphasizing that through each transition, we remain steadfast and supportive, both for loved ones and for ourselves. The poem highlights the importance of patience and confidence, suggesting that one should not fret during challenging times but instead find solace in contemplating nature and its struggles. The imagery of winter trees, stark and bare, enduring the cold winter wind and frost, serves as a metaphor for the difficult periods in life. Similarly, the description of summer's heat turning green to brown, with leaves and plants wilting and falling to the ground, represents the inevitable hardships and losses we face. However, the poem reassures us that just as the roots of plants remain steadfast and wait for a time of change, we too can find strength and resilience within ourselves. The arrival of warmth and rain, which allows the roots to sustain and bring vibrant colors back to the plants, symbolizes the renewal and growth that follows difficult times. This cyclical process of change and renewal is a natural part of life, and the commitment to remaining steadfast through it all is a testament to our resilience. In essence, "I Shall Remain" is a reflection on the importance of resilience, patience, and steadfastness in navigating life's challenges. It reminds us that, like the roots of plants, we have the strength to endure and thrive through the cycles of change. The poem encourages us to remain confident and patient, knowing that life's cycles will bring sustenance and renewal in due time. This reflection underscores the poem's message that resilience and steadfastness are key to weathering life's storms and emerging stronger on the other side.

PRACTICAL EXERCISES
Resilience and Support

JOURNALING PROMPT:

Describe a challenging period you have endured. What "roots" or supports helped you remain steadfast? How do you nurture them?

VISUALIZATION EXERCISE

Imagine yourself as a tree weathering the seasons. With each breath, visualize your roots growing stronger and deeper.

REFLECTION QUESTION:

How can you support loved ones during their seasons of change while caring for your own well-being?

A DAILY CYCLE OF THE TRINITY

The body benefits from movement, and the mind benefits from stillness."

— Sakyong Mipham

As night ends, the body wakes—eyes open, setting the path the mind will take.

Transcending awareness — the show seen on stage, moving beyond its curtain to find the hidden mind to engage.

Journey toward the chosen door, as negative doors close behind.

Manifesting and engaging senses once the door opens to what I choose to find.

Guidance of the mind's eye to what it sees creates calmness, putting mind at ease.

In this state, I shall find the noise of the world and past experiences left behind.

Now the path is clear to reflect upon my qualities, internal wealth what I value most of myself.

Self-affirmations and manifestation to attract positive energy, for this will determine what the universe will give back to me.

To contemplate, I am more than self, a part of something vast, the web of energy of the universe itself.

Like a grain of sand on an ocean shore, my energy but a fragment intertwined in its infinite design.

To contemplate vigor, vitality, and health, I shall visualize the desired energy itself.

Breath shall set the cadence for manifesting good health, for this is life's true wealth.

With inhalation, the visualization of energy is golden and bright, saturating and creating immense health of body and mind.

Exhalation drives the elimination of disease and negative energy. Outward flow with dark red glow never to return.

Now for the physical of the trinity, continuous body in motion, creating strength, vigor, and vitality.

The cycle will continuously be ingrained in the mind, attracting positive energy over time.

Persistent practice to improve physical health — remember this is life's true wealth..

REFLECTION

The poem "Daily Cycle of the Trinity" was written to capture the holistic approach to well-being, emphasizing the interconnections of mind, body, and spirit. It begins with the awakening of the body, setting the stage for the mind's journey toward awareness and engagement. This initial transition highlights the importance of starting the day with a clear and focused mind, ready to embrace the opportunities and challenges ahead. The poem then delves into the process of calming the mind, guiding it towards a state of tranquility where the noise of the world and past experiences are left behind. This clear path allows for self-reflection, focusing on one's internal qualities and values. The practice of self-affirmation and manifestation is emphasized as a means to attract positive energy, reinforcing the idea that our thoughts and intentions shape our reality. The contemplation of being part of something vast, the web of energy of the universe, underscores the interconnections of all things. This perspective fosters a sense of humility and gratitude, recognizing that our individual energy is but a fragment of the infinite design. The poem encourages visualization of desired energy, particularly in terms of vigor, vitality, and health, which are seen as life's true wealth. Breathing is presented as a fundamental practice for manifesting good health. The visualization of golden, bright energy during inhalation symbolizes the intake of positive, life-sustaining energy, while the exhalation of dark red glow represents the elimination of disease and negative energy.

This cyclical process of breathing reinforces the importance of mindfulness and intentionality in maintaining physical and mental well-being. The poem concludes by emphasizing the physical aspect of the trinity, highlighting the importance of continuous motion and physical activity in creating strength, vigor, and vitality. The cycle of mind, body, and spirit is ingrained in the mind, creating and attracting positive energy over time. Persistence in practicing these principles is key to improving physical health and achieving a balanced, fulfilling life. In essence, "Daily Cycle of the Trinity" is a reflection on the holistic approach to well-being, emphasizing the importance of mindfulness, self-reflection, and physical activity. It reminds us that by nurturing our mind, body, and spirit, we can create a positive and fulfilling life, grounded in the interconnections of all things. This reflection underscores the poem's message that true wealth lies in the health and vitality of our entire being.

Mind-Body-Spirit Integration

JOURNALING PROMPT

How do you currently nurture your mind, body, and spirit? Which area might need more attention?

BREATH VISUALIZATION

Try the poem's guided visualization. With each inhale, imagine golden energy filling you; with each exhale, release negativity and tension.

REFLECTION QUESTION

What daily rituals help you connect to your inner strengths and maintain balance?

APPENDIX
Quotes & Inspirations

The following appendix gathers quotes and inspirations from authors and thinkers whose wisdom I found especially impactful and relevant to each poem. I share them here in the hope that they may offer you the same light and encouragement they gave to me.

"Love does not consist in gazing at each other, but in looking outward together in the same direction."

— Antoine de Saint-Exupéry

Antoine de Saint-Exupéry (1900–1944) was a French writer, poet, and pioneering aviator. Best known for *The Little Prince*, his works explore themes of love, responsibility, and human connection. This quote reflects the poem's theme of two lives uniting in shared purpose and mutual uplift.

"The most precious gift we can offer anyone is our attention."

— Thich Nhat Hanh

Thich Nhat Hanh (1926–2022) was a Vietnamese Buddhist monk, peace activist, and global teacher of mindfulness. His words emphasize that attention is the deepest form of love. This perfectly echoes the poem's call to be present and mindful in relationships, especially when love is expressed through selfless acts.

∼ • ∽

"What you do speaks so loudly that I cannot hear what you say."

— Ralph Waldo Emerson

Ralph Waldo Emerson (1803–1882) was an American essayist, lecturer, and poet, central to the Transcendentalist movement. He taught the importance of integrity and action over empty words. This idea resonates with the poem's message that commitment, patience, and consistent actions sustain a lasting union.

∼ • ∽

"Between stimulus and response there is a space. In that space is our power to choose our response."

— Viktor E. Frankl

Viktor Frankl (1905–1997) was an Austrian neurologist, psychiatrist, and Holocaust survivor. Author of *Man's Search for Meaning*, he founded logotherapy, which emphasizes finding meaning even in suffering. His insight on the space between stimulus and response mirrors the poem's teaching of mindful speech and thoughtful action.

∼ • ∽

"You have power over your mind — not outside events. Realize this, and you will find strength."

— Marcus Aurelius

Marcus Aurelius (121–180 CE) was a Roman emperor and Stoic philosopher. His writings in *Meditations* are a cornerstone of Stoic philosophy. His reminder that the mind is within our control aligns with the poem's theme of breaking free from negative self-talk and reclaiming inner strength through presence and positivity.

∼ • ∽

"I can be changed by what happens to me. But I refuse to be reduced by it."

— Maya Angelou

Maya Angelou (1928–2014) was an American poet, singer, dancer, activist, and memoirist, celebrated for works like *I Know Why the Caged Bird Sings*. Her resilience and wisdom inspire generations. Her words reinforce the poem's imagery of roots enduring seasons — remaining steadfast through life's cycles.

∽ • ∾

"The body benefits from movement, and the mind benefits from stillness."

— Sakyong Mipham

Sakyong Mipham (b. 1962) is a Tibetan lama and head of the Shambhala Buddhist lineage. His teaching that body and mind need different nourishment aligns with the poem's vision of harmony across mind, body, and spirit.

∽ • ∾

AFTERWORD

As you reach the end of this collection, I want to extend my heartfelt thanks for allowing these poems and reflections to accompany you.

Sharing these pieces has been a deeply personal journey of facing my own doubts, celebrating moments of connection, and finding purpose through the act of writing itself. Each poem was born from a desire not only to understand myself but to reach out and support others who are navigating their own paths of self-betterment. The themes of gratitude, purpose, mindfulness, presence, and resilience weave throughout these pages. I hope that, however you experience them, they encourage you to pause, reflect, and practice kindness toward yourself and those around you. Progress, I have learned, is rarely a straight line. There are days of doubt and days of joy, but every moment is a chance to begin again — to remain steadfast like the roots in winter, to shine a light for others, or simply to breathe and be present. I am grateful to my mother, whose unwavering love and quiet strength continue to inspire me. I am grateful to you, the reader, for your openness and courage to explore these reflections. May you continue your journey with compassion and curiosity. May you find light in connection and purpose in presence. And may these words remain a gentle anchor whenever you need them most. With gratitude and encouragement,

Michael VJ Connelly

ACKNOWLEDGMENTS

This collection would not have been possible without the encourage- ment, insight, and support of many individuals and communities. I extend my heartfelt thanks to:

My family, especially my mother, Silvana Ludovici, my wife, Ilsy, and my sister, Linda, for their enduring love, resilience, and the inspiration they have provided throughout my life.

To all readers and supporters who engage with these words and share their own paths of self-betterment — your openness and courage inspire and sustain this work.

Thank you for being part of this journey. Your presence and encouragement have made all the difference.

ABOUT THE AUTHOR

Michael VJ Connelly is an advocate for personal growth, reflection, and mindfulness. With over 20 years of leadership experience in healthcare, he has dedicated himself to navigating challenges with compassion and clarity. But beyond his career, his deeper journey has been personal — learning how to pause, breathe, think, and separate past events from the emotions that once held him captive. His writing became the anchor for rediscovering joy, gratitude, and self- betterment. Today, Michael embraces his identity as a "human pilot," navigating life with the poems in this book as anchors along his path. *Self: A Reflective Collection of Poems for Self-Betterment* is both a personal testimony and an offering to others — a reminder that while pain and turbulence are part of the journey, love, resilience, and heritage can light the way forward.

Pause, Read, Reflect.

www.ingramcontent.com/pod-product-compliance
Lightning Source LLC
Chambersburg PA
CBHW050905120626

46554CB00003B/1015